Purb

~ *a brief g*

Inspiring Places Publishing

2 Down Lodge Close
Alderholt
Fordingbridge
Hants..

SP6 3JA

ISBN 978-0-9564104-1-2

© 2009 Robert Westwood
All rights reserved

Maps by Jennifer Westwood

Printed by Corvette Consultancy, Bournemouth

Contents

Page:

3   Introduction

4   Landscape and Geology

9   History

12   Places to Visit

27   Suggested Walks

33   Purbeck Beaches

36   Map of Places to See

37   Hidden Purbeck

40   Other tourist attractions and useful information

Other titles by *Inspiring Places Publishing:*

Fossils and Rocks of the Jurassic Coast
The Jurassic Coast Illustrated
Ancient Dorset
Dark Age Dorset
Historic Dorset
Smugglers' Dorset
The Life and Works of Thomas Hardy
Mysterious Places of Dorset
Day Tours in the East of Dorset
Mystery Big Cats of Dorset

Buy online at www.inspiringplaces.co.uk

JURASSICCOAST
**QUALITY
BUSINESS**

Introduction

Purbeck is a unique place, not strictly speaking an island, but certainly a place with a distinct character. For those seeking a relaxing holiday or an enjoyable day out it has a lot to offer; a stunning coastline, safe, sandy beaches, quaint villages, historic sites and miles of scenic walks. There is lots of accommodation, from luxury hotels to cheerful b&bs, from spacious cottages to caravans by the sea.

This is a brief guide on what Purbeck has to offer. It explains the landscape and its geology, gives a short account of the rich history of the area and describes the main places of interest. There are lists of suggested things to do at each location, recommendations for some interesting walks and advice about where to eat and drink. There is a guide to the varied and beautiful beaches of Purbeck as well as lots of practical information.

Note: The area covered by this guide forms the administrative district of Purbeck. Traditionally the term the "Isle of Purbeck" refers to a smaller area.

Landscape and Geology

Purbeck's unique landscape owes its beauty to its underlying geology. Layers of rock from the Jurassic and Cretaceous periods trend parallel to the coast and have been gracefully folded by compression in a north-south direction as two plates of the Earth's crust collided; the same tectonic upheaval that produced the mountains of the Alps. Two relatively hard layers, the Portland and Purbeck limestones and the Chalk, sandwich softer clays, silts and sands, resulting in twin ridges with a rich, productive vale between. From Peveril Point at Swanage to St. Aldhelm's Head the coast is formed from the hard limestones; as it sweeps northwards around the headland softer, older Jurassic sediments are revealed until the limestones reappear at Worbarrow. The Chalk ridge forms the northern boundary of the Isle of Purbeck. In the east it is revealed in the formidable cliffs around Ballard Down with the sea stacks of Old Harry and his family providing well-known landmarks. As we travel westwards the hard limestones and the Chalk edge closer together, squeezing the softer Cretaceous sediments between them. In the far west of Purbeck, at Durdle Door, they meet, the limestones continue below sea level and the Chalk once more forms impressive cliffs.

It is not just the landscape that has been shaped by the geology, human endeavour has been influenced and determined by it. The limestones have been the source of a wonderful building stone that for long periods ensured the economic stability of the region. The fact that they lie in gently sloping layers along the coast has facilitated their quarrying and export by ship. The gentle sweep of Swanage Bay, cut out of the softer sediments between the two harder rocks, has led to the development of a thriving seaside town with a safe beach. The twin ridges of high ground proved convenient for the army to practise its gunnery; they continue to use large areas today and the inconvenience to the visitor is perhaps negated by the splendidly protected and un-commercialised landscape that is revealed when the ranges are open.

Today Purbeck's coastline is part of the Jurassic Coast, England's only natural World Heritage Site. The oldest rocks are the Jurassic clays and silts of Kimmeridge Bay, formed in a Jurassic sea teeming with life. The limestones of the Portland and Purbeck, the youngest Jurassic rocks, represent a shallower, tropical sea and even freshwater lagoons nestling along the ancient shoreline. In these lagoons dinosaurs roamed and many of their footprints have been found in the Purbeck quarries and along the coast. Following on from these, the early Cretaceous rocks, the soft sands and clays of Swanage Bay are largely sediments from a huge river delta. The sea returned again to prompt the deposition of the Chalk, a rock composed almost entirely of the tiny calcareous shells of microscopic organisms that sank to the bottom of the warm, tropical Cretaceous sea – a staggering illustration of geological time when you look at the mighty white cliffs that mark the end of the Jurassic coast.

Things to see on the coast:

Handfast Point – These impressive chalk cliffs mark the end of the Jurassic Coast. They are, in fact, the youngest Cretaceous rocks. It was at this moment in time that the Earth probably suffered a huge meteorite impact that resulted in the extinction of most life on the planet, including the dinosaurs and ammonites. The sea stacks of Old Harry and his family are erosional features.

Landscape and Geology

Peveril Point, Swanage – South of Peveril Ponit is the gentle sweep of Durlston Bay with the classic section of Purbeck Beds, mostly freshwater sediments from forested lagoons rich in life, including many dinosaurs. Their footprints are occasionally found here. Just off Peveril Point and well exposed at low tide is a plunging syncline, a trough-like fold in the Purbeck strata.

Durlston Head – The cliffs of this lovely country park are Portland Stone. Old quarry workings can be seen at Tilly Whim caves. The Great Globe [above] just below the Victorian castle was commissioned by George Burt, weighs 40 tons and is carved from Portland Stone.

Above: The Purbeck coast at Winspit: The Portland Stone was quarried here well into the 20th century.

Winspit – More quarries in the Portland Stone; the vast caves show how thick some of the layers are, ideal for building stone. Look out for the giant ammonite Titanites in the rocks near the sea.

St Aldhelm's Head - Chapman's Pool – Again the Portland Stone is the foundation for this spectacular headland: on the western side of it lies Chapman's Pool cut out of softer and older Jurassic rocks. Hounstout cliff the other side of the bay shows a sequence of Jurassic strata representing a gradual shallowing of the ancient sea with the limestones forming a resistant cap at the top.

Kimmeridge – The rocks here are marine Jurassic sediments, rich in fossils of the many animals that lived in the warm, shallow seas. The thin layers show how the environment changed with time, often in a periodic manner. It is in these strata that decaying organic matter has resulted in oil reserves under the North Sea where they are deeply buried.

Worbarrow Bay – Almost a mirror image of Swanage Bay, except the soft rocks between the Portland/Purbeck limestones and the Chalk have been squeezed and thinned.

Lulworth Cove – Perhaps the most well-known location on the Purbeck coast, Lulworth presents a similar picture to Worbarrow. The sea has broken through the hard limestones and scoured away the softer sands and clays behind, before stopping at the hard chalk. It is a feature typical of a "concordant" coastline where the strata and the coast run parallel. Look out for the Lulworth Crumple, tight folds in the Purbeck strata at Stair Hole caused by the Alpine earth movements which tilted and folded all the Purbeck rocks.

Above: Chapman's Pool with Houns-tout behind. Below: The chapel at St. Aldhelm's Head and right: Inside the chapel.

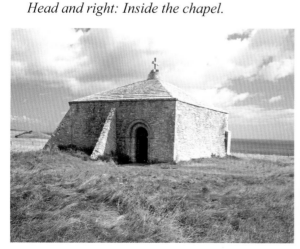

Landscape and Geology

The Portland Stone

It is the thick, homogeneous layers that make the Portland Stone such a fine building stone. This is an "oolitic" limestone, made of millions of ooliths, tiny balls of calcium carbonate, precipitated out of seawater and rolled backwards and forwards by the action of an ancient, shallow, tropical sea.

The Portland Stone at Seacombe near Worth Matravers.

History

There is much of historical interest in Purbeck, and it is not possible here to give a detailed account. What follows is a brief outline of some of the events in Purbeck's colourful history and the places associated with them.

Dorset is well-known for its Iron Age hillforts. Defence against a mighty foreign empire was not their purpose, rather protection against similarly armed ambitious neighbours. They provided little deterrence for the Roman army and all were quickly overrun in AD 43. There were battles at some [like Maiden Castle and Hod Hill] but others probably capitulated without a fight. It is not known what happened at Flower's Barrow overlooking Worbarrow Bay, but ghostly legends involving marching soldiers suggest there may have been at least a skirmish! There can be few hillforts with as spectacular a position.

Little is known of Purbeck's history in the centuries following the Roman withdrawal, but in Saxon times it became an important part of the kingdom of Wessex. Wareham was fortified by Alfred the Great as defence against the Vikings and Corfe Castle was also a major stronghold. Wareham was occupied by the Danish king, Guthrum in

History

Below: St. Mary's Church and the River Frome at Wareham.

AD 877, but fortune favoured the Saxons when the Danish fleet, on its way to attack Exeter, was largely destroyed by a storm just off Peveril Point, Swanage. A column on Swanage seafront, capped with Russian cannonballs, commemorates a "victory" by Alfred the Great. Today you can walk around the banks that mark the old Saxon defences of Wareham, and perched on top of the bank as you enter Wareham from the north is the Saxon church of St. Martin, one of the few remaining Saxon churches in Dorset.

In AD 978 a deed was committed at Corfe Castle that even shocked an Anglo-Saxon world used to violence. The young King Edward, son of Edgar who had presided over a brief golden age of Wessex, was brutally murdered by followers of his step-mother Aelfthryth; probably on her orders but this has never been established. It led to her son Aethelred becoming king. Known to history as "the Unready", he presided over a time of increased Viking attacks and was forced to pay huge sums of "Danegeld" to buy them off. Stories and legends grew up about the dead king and he was later canonised. The body of "Edward the Martyr" was eventually taken to Shaftesbury Abbey which consequently grew rich as a place of pilgrimage.

In medieval times Corfe Castle grew in importance. It was greatly extended by King John who loved to hunt in the Purbeck forests. The area witnessed much bloodshed during the civil war between King Stephen and the Empress Matilda in the 12th century, with both Corfe and

Wareham castles being besieged by the king. Corfe Castle was again besieged in the English Civil War in 1643 and 1645/6. The defence of the castle by Royalists under the command of Lady Bankes has become legend. The castle was only taken through an act of betrayal; the fortifications had proved so formidable that the ruins you see today are the result of demolition by the Parliamentarians to ensure they could not be used in the future.

Any visitor to Purbeck can hardly fail to notice that stone has been an important part of its economy. Quarries are everywhere on the coast and on the high ground inland; the Purbeck limestones have been quarried here since Roman times. Many different layers of rock have been quarried for different purposes, but some simple distinctions can be made. The coastal quarries extracted Portland Stone. This oolitic limestone is possibly the world's best building stone and has been used in many of London's great buildings including St. Paul's Cathedral. The inland quarries work various Purbeck limestones. These are younger than the Portland Stone and were typically formed in freshwater lagoons. They make excellent decorative stone and paving stone. Quarries are still being worked and much stone has been provided for the restoration of medieval buildings, including Salisbury Cathedral. The Purbeck Marble is a particularly fine decorative stone. It is not, however, a true marble which is a metamorphic rock, but it can be polished as a true marble can.

History

Above left: The Saxon church of St. Martin's at Wareham sits on top of the old Saxon town walls.
Right: The quarried cliffs at Dancing Ledge.

Places to Visit

Wareham

Wareham, the gateway to Purbeck, is an historic and unique town. It was probably an important settlement in Roman times, connected via the River Frome and Poole Harbour to the Roman port at Hamworthy. Purbeck was an important industrial region in Roman times with the quarrying of Purbeck Marble, the manufacture of jewellery at Kimmeridge and a thriving pottery industry using the local clays from the north of the region.

Wareham was a key defensive "burgh" in Saxon times, its town walls built on the orders of Alfred the Great against the ever present threat of Viking raids. Today you can walk around those walls although they are now grassy banks. The Saxon church of St. Martin's [page 10] is thought to stand on the site of an older church founded by St. Aldhelm, the famous Saxon scholar and first Bishop of Sherborne. Inside is an effigy of T.E. Lawrence, intended originally for Westminster Abbey, and striking medieval wall paintings. After the Conquest the Normans recognised its strategic importance and built a castle here. In 1138 it saw action in the civil war between King Stephen and the Empress Matilda.

Throughout much of its remaining history Wareham has been a busy little market town, its importance as a port gradually declining as ships grew too big to navigate the Frome. Today it continues to thrive although a sizeable proportion of its prosperity depends on the tourist trade.

Things to do:

- Walk the Saxon town walls.
- Visit St. Martin's Church.
- Visit the town museum.
- Walk along the river bank.
- Have something to eat or drink at one of the places on the town quay.

Below: The River Frome at Wareham; the castle was on the hill on the right.

Corfe Castle

One of the best known villages in the whole of England, Corfe Castle sits in the centre of Purbeck by a natural gap in the Chalk ridge. Two streams have combined to leave a central knoll which is an ideal and obvious place for a castle. It seems likely that there was a wooden structure here quite early in Saxon times and it was, perhaps, an important line in the defence against Viking raiders. It was a royal residence in later Saxon times and was the scene of the brutal murder of the young King Edward in 978. As mentioned elsewhere this crime had immense repercussions. The Normans gradually enlarged the castle and it became of major importance. It saw a number of sieges; during the civil war between King Stephen and the Empress Matilda, in the conflict between King Henry III and his barons and finally in the English Civil War.

Today Corfe Castle is an enchanting little village, although seldom quiet. In summer it attracts hordes of tourists, but there is plenty of space within the castle grounds. As you enter the village on the road from Wareham there is a little lane on the left, right next to the castle hill; up here a little way is a free car park for walkers, and it is a relatively short stroll to the village. Near the beginning of this road there is a short,

Below: Corfe Castle from the Chalk ridge to the east.

Places to Visit

but steep path up on to the ridge from where there are fabulous views of the castle. If you want to get away from the crowds and admire the castle and its magnificent site, this is the place.

As well as the castle and National Trust shop Corfe has another attraction just off the main square, the model village. This is also an excellent place to stop for a bite to eat.

Not so well-known is Corfe Common. As you leave the village towards Swanage there is a turning on the right to Kingston. Up this road on the right is Corfe Common. You can usually park in a small space by the roadside and the common is another great place to stroll and admire views of the castle. It is also great for dogs!

Things to do:
- Visit the castle and National Trust shop.
- Climb the ridge to view the castle. [either east or west]
- Explore the village.
- Visit the model village. [good restaurant]
- Walk on Corfe Common.

Below: Corfe Castle viewed from Corfe Common, taken on a frosty morning.

Studland

The extended village of Studland lies to the north of Swanage in the shelter of the Chalk ridge. Perhaps not pretty or quaint in the manner of Kingston or Worth Matravers, it boasts several beautiful and accessible beaches, ideal for bathing. The beaches are owned and run by the National Trust. At Knoll Beach there is a visitor centre with a popular beach café. The calm waters of the bay and the gently shelving beach have proved useful to many groups over the years. It was once a favoured location for pirates to anchor, who dared not risk being trapped by the narrow entrance to Poole Harbour. Likewise smugglers found it useful to bring their contraband ashore here, hide it among the dunes and then transport it over the neighbouring heathland to markets inland. During the Second World War it was used as a training ground for troops prior to the D-Day landings.

At South Beach stands the well-known Bankes Arms, a pub reputedly dating from the 16th century. It has a delightful garden overlooking the bay and is the perfect place to end a walk. In the 19th century it was run by William Lawrence, a veteran of the Napoleonic wars. His grave is by the porch of the nearby Norman church of St. Nicholas and it is worth a visit. The details of William's career are astonishing. He fought at all the major battles including Waterloo, even surviving being a member of the "Forlorn Hope" at one battle, the group of volunteers who were the first to storm defences. It is a short, easy walk from here to Handfast Point with Old Harry rock. The views over Poole Harbour and Bournemouth are breathtaking and a short walk south over the headland rewards with equally impressive views over Swanage Bay.

West of Studland is a remnant of once widespread heathland. Sitting in the middle of one of the main paths across is the Agglestone, a huge boulder of ironstone that is the natural product of the erosion of softer rocks below in the geological succession. According to legend it was thrown by the devil from the Isle of Wight; aiming for Corfe Castle, he missed and it landed here. I have never heard an explanation of why he wanted to demolish Corfe Castle!

Things to do:

- Sandy beaches are good for swimming, visitor centre at Knoll Beach has a lovely waterside café.
- Visit the Bankes Arms and Norman church at South Beach.
- Walk to Handfast Point and Old Harry. [see page 27]
- Walk across the heath to the Agglestone.

Places to Visit

Above: The village of Studland from the Chalk ridge to the south. The bay was once a favoured mooring for pirates.

Swanage

Swanage is an ancient settlement that appears in the Domesday Book, but it was in the 19th century that it became popular as a seaside resort, following the completion of the railway link to Wareham. Two great Victorian entrepreneurs did much to put Swanage on the map, John Mowlem and his nephew George Burt. Mowlem started the great construction company that bears his name; both worked in the stone industry and their company was responsible for much rebuilding in Victorian London. They were great benefactors of Swanage and brought a great deal of the old stonework they replaced back to Dorset. Thus the town hall of Swanage boasts a front that was once the façade of the Mercer's Hall in the city of London. The Purbeck House Hotel was built as a residence for George Burt and contains many recycled pieces of London stonework.

Peveril Point is at the southern end of Swanage Bay and is a hazardous place for boats as treacherous ledges stretch out to sea. You can follow the cliff up the side of Durlston Bay to the country park at **Durlston Head**. This was created by George Burt and has spectacular views of the Purbeck coast. It is a haven for wild life and wild flowers. There is a very informative visitor centre and regular events are hosted. The area of park above Peveril Point is a great place for a picnic and has wonderful views over the town and bay.

In the centre of town is Swanage Station, home of the Swanage Railway. Thanks to the efforts of George Burt the line from Wareham to Swanage was opened in 1885. It was closed in 1972 but thanks to volunteers the track was restored and a steam and diesel service to Corfe Castle has now been operating for many years. In 2009 a service to Wareham was re-opened, so, once again, it is possible to travel by train from London to Swanage.

Things to do:

- The lovely, sandy beach provides safe bathing.
- Visit the Heritage Centre.
- Walk to Peveril Point.
- Visit Durlston Country Park.
- Take a trip on the steam railway.
- Coincide your trip with one of Swanage's many festivals.

Places to Visit

*Left and above:
The sheltered bay
and sandy beach at
Swanage provide
traditional, family
seaside entertainment.*

Worth Matravers

This pretty little village is justifiably well-known. With houses built of mellow Purbeck stone, a village green with duck pond and an atmospheric traditional pub, it is a lovely base from which to explore the surrounding countryside and coast. There are two car parks which politely request a modest donation to their upkeep at GR SY 973777 and SY 963774. From the first, at the entrance to the village, it is a short stroll down to the coast at Winspit. Here huge caverns have been driven into the Portland Stone which was loaded onto barges and then onto larger ships at Swanage. It is now a peaceful and beautiful place and the old quarry workings have left convenient ledges for the tourist to sit and enjoy the view.

From the second car park it is a short, level walk to the cliffs overlooking Chapman's Pool. The view westwards along the Dorset coast is quite breathtaking. Beware that if you want to walk round to St. Aldhelm's Head from here there is a very steep descent and following ascent to negotiate. There is, alternatively, a level walk to St. Aldhelm's Head from the car park along a gravel track. The views from here are well worth the effort! There is a curious Norman chapel on St. Aldhelm's Head. A sturdy, square building with one window it seems a strange setting for a place of worship. It is dedicated to the 7th century saint who was the first Bishop of Sherborne; he had built a number of chapels around his diocese and there may well have been such an early construction here. It is still used and has become quite a popular wedding venue.

The parish church of St. Nicholas was begun in the 11th century but was extensively restored in Victorian times. Side by side in the

Right: The quarried cliffs at Winspit - a great place to picnic and to sit and soak up the sun!

Above: The village pond at Worth Matravers, with, behind, some of the cottages made of the local Purbeck stone. Worth is very popular with walkers, with easy access to the coast, convenient and cheap car parking and a great pub!

graveyard lie the graves of Benjamin Jesty and his wife Elizabeth. In 1774 Jesty achieved local notoriety in his home town of Yetminster by deliberately infecting his wife and two sons with cowpox via a darning needle. He did this because he believed it would lead to immunity from deadly smallpox which was widespread at the time. He was proved right and is now generally accepted as being one of the pioneers of vaccination, preceding Edward Jenner by some twenty years.

Another important scientific achievement associated with Worth is radar. During the Second World War the coast here became a testing ground for the new radar technology. A memorial on St. Aldhelm's Head commemorates this.

Things to do:
- Sit outside the Square and Compass.
- Visit the church.
- Walk to Winspit. [see page 30]
- Walk to St. Aldhelm's Head.

Kingston

This small, quaint village offers some of the best views of Corfe Castle, particularly from the garden of the village pub, the Scott Arms. There can be few better places to enjoy a drink or meal on a warm, summer's evening. Kingston is dominated by the younger of its two churches, an elaborate and imposing building of Purbeck stone. The older church situated on the road out of the village towards Swanage, was built by the first Lord Eldon who owned the Encombe estate. The newer church was built by the third Lord Eldon.

The road past the Scott Arms ends at a small car park from which it is a relatively short climb up to Swyre Head. The views east and west along the coast from here are magnificent. From the woods just behind the church there is a level path which leads to the top of Houns-tout cliff. Again the views are stunning, particularly over St. Aldhelm's Head and the little bay of Chapman's Pool. It also offers a good view of the Encombe estate nestling in the "Golden Bowl".

Things to do:

- Sit in the garden of the Scott Arms and admire one of the best views of Corfe Castle.
- See the "new" church.
- Walk to Swyre Head. [see page 32]
- Walk to Houns-tout.

Below: The Scott Arms - is there a better pub garden? The perfect place to relax after a good walk.

Kimmeridge

One of the key locations on the Jurassic Coast, Kimmeridge is justifiably famous for its geology. The black shales and harder bands of limestone were formed in an ancient Jurassic sea teeming with life, hence the profusion of fossils in these cliffs. The thin, gently dipping layers of sediments show how the Jurassic environment changed over the millions of years it took for the rocks to accumulate.

The bay is owned by the Smedmore estate and a toll is payable to reach the large grassy car park overlooking the bay. It is a great place for a picnic. There is not much of a beach but plenty of rock pools to explore. Although the water is shallow and calm, you need to be aware of the rock ledges when swimming. Kimmeridge is a favourite place for snorkelling and has been designated part of the Purbeck Marine Wildlife Reserve. There is an interesting Marine Centre at the bay.

On the headland at the eastern end of the bay stands the well-known folly, Clavell Tower, now a holiday apartment. It was built in the 1820s by Reverend John Richards who had inherited the estate. Some say its intended use was as a summer house, but coastal structures built around this time which commanded extensive

views along the coast have always suggested more illicit connections. A large percentage of the population was involved in smuggling at this time and it is quite possible that landowners and others in "higher" levels of society were involved.

Kimmeridge has a long history of commercial activity, or at least attempted commercial activity. In Roman times a hard band of shale was cut and polished to make jewellery.

At times enterprising individuals have tried to make use of the organic content in the shales at Kimmeridge. Producing lamp oil was one such venture that failed, due to the pungent smell it produced. In the 19th century the hard, black shale was mined to produce oil and gas and these workings can still be made out at Clavell's Hard.

Kimmeridge has what is possibly the oldest working oil well in the world, marked by the famous nodding donkey behind the cliffs. This can cause some confusion. The oil is not from the shale exposed in the bay but from older, deeper Jurassic rocks. However, the Kimmeridge layers are the source of the North Sea oil where they are buried deep under the sea.

Things to do:

- Explore the rock pools.
- Picnic overlooking the bay.
- Visit the Marine Centre.
- Go snorkelling.
- Visit Clavell's Café and Farm Shop.
- Walk up on the cliffs by Clavell Tower.

Top: Looking across Kimmeridge Bay from the foot of Hen Cliff.

Tyneham

Much has been written about the abandoned village of Tyneham. It has come to represent, in many people's minds, a symbol of lost, rural England; a small community dependent on traditional trades, where life was hard but the setting tranquil and beautiful. The sacrifice of the villagers who left it in 1943 not only helped the war effort, but has, perhaps inadvertently, preserved a corner of "old England" for the benefit of future generations.

It was shortly before Christmas in 1943 that the village was requisitioned by the army for training purposes. Huge forces were being massed for D-Day and the region's ridges, valleys and beaches offered perfect territory for their preparation. Without complaint the villagers left, hoping to return after the war. They never did so and the army uses the area to this day. However, it is open to the public most weekends and throughout school holidays, and it has to be said that the continued presence of the army has led to the area being conserved and becoming a unique visitor experience.

It is a truly beautiful setting, nestled in the valley between the Chalk ridge and Purbeck limestone ridge. A mile away is lovely Worbarrow Bay, carved out of the softer Cretaceous rocks that underlie

Below: The village church of St. Mary's at Tyneham.

Places to Visit

Places to Visit

Above: A row of cottages at Tyneham.

the village with mighty Chalk cliffs on one side and a limestone headland on the other. You can wander around the ruined cottages and visit the carefully preserved church and the school house which has been turned into a charming museum. There is a large car park which requests a small donation. Even at the height of the summer holidays, although quite busy, it always seems peaceful. The beach at Worbarrow is an easy walk away and, all in all, it is a perfect place to spend a day relaxing, picnicking, swimming and soaking up the atmosphere. Just don't tell too many people about it!

Things to do:
- Explore the deserted village.
- Visit the church and the school house.
- Walk down to Worbarrow Bay.
- Have a picnic.

Lulworth Cove

There is evidence of Bronze Age and Iron Age occupation near Lulworth and a Roman grave has been found nearby. Lulworth was a relatively thriving community at the time of Domesday; the name is clearly of Saxon origin, meaning the land or enclosure belonging to Lulla. There seems little doubt its unique, sheltered harbour would have been valued through the ages.

The formation of the cove is something thousands of visiting students have been lectured about. It is all down to the structure of the rocks along the Purbeck coast. The strata trend parallel to the coast, with soft sands and clays being sandwiched between harder layers of the Chalk and the Purbeck and Portland limestones. A river has broken through the limestones, allowing the sea to scour out the softer rocks behind, before coming up against the harder Chalk. If you look at the Portland and Purbeck strata near the mouth of the cove you will see that the layers are dipping steeply, in fact they are almost vertical. This is because they are part of a giant fold formed during the Alpine mountain building episode. The softer sands and clays and the Chalk are younger and lie on top of the Portland and Purbeck rocks, and they once came up and over the limestones in a great step like fold. What we see now at Lulworth is the vertical part of the step.

The range walks to the east of the cove are only open during the school holidays and most weekends. When they are it is just a short walk along the ridge to the east of the cove to the Fossil Forest. This is clearly signposted and some steps lead down to a ledge above the sea where the fossilised remains of tree stumps can be clearly seen. More accurately they are the remains of tree stumps that were colonised by algae as they died, forming what are known as stromatolites. It is thought that this ancient tropical forest was once a coastal swamp where dinosaurs roamed and that a sudden rise in sea level led to the death of the forest and its colonisation by algae.

Places to Visit

Durdle Door at dusk.

Another must see at Lulworth is Stair Hole on the other side of the cove. This is another cove in the making; the sea has again broken through the limestones and is beginning to scour out behind. Exposed on the eastern side of the Hole is the famous "Lulworth Crumple", a series of folds in the Purbeck strata caused by great earth movements.

The Heritage Centre in the middle of the village has an excellent display explaining the local geology and is well worth a visit.

There is a large car park next to the Heritage Centre and from here you will see lots of people making their way up the coastal path to the west. This steep climb leads to Durdle Door, one of the most famous landmarks on the south coast. This natural arch has been

formed as the sea has exploited weaker cracks and joints in the Purbeck limestones; such joints are a common feature of rock strata that have been uplifted and folded. It is possible to park nearer at Durdle Door holiday park. If you don't mind walking a little there is free road parking on the outskirts of Lulworth on the road that leads up past the church.

Things to do:

- Visit the fossil forest. [When range walks are open.]
- Have a look at Stair Hole and the Lulworth Crumple.
- Walk to Durdle Door.
- Enjoy the beach.
- Visit the Heritage Centre.

Above: The Lulworth Crumple.
Below: Lulworth Cove.

Suggested Walks

The walks detailed in this section all have lots of interest. They include parts of the stunning Jurassic Coast, nature reserves, historical sites and areas of outstanding natural beauty. All are based on places to eat and drink; Purbeck has some famous, atmospheric pubs. They are all fairly short walks which can easily be completed in a morning or afternoon, and generally there is much to interest children. They are suitable for dogs but be aware that in places there may be animals grazing and there are places with precipitous drops. In dry weather there may also be little water en route. The grid reference for the start and finish point is given at the start of each walk. The maps are intended as rough guides, you are strongly advised to use OS Explorer sheet OL15.

Walk 1 - Studland - Handfast Point

This walk starts and finishes at the lovely **Bankes Arms** next to the National Trust car park [paying] at South Beach. Walk down the hill past the pub and turn left at the bottom [by public conveniences]. Follow the path all the way to the headland of Handfast Point. Here there are tremendous views of Poole Harbour and Old Harry and his family of stacks. Follow the cliff path to the right and climb the hill. At the top ignore the first sign to the right [Purbeck Way] and carry on a little to enjoy views over Swanage Bay. Keep to the right and you will

Walks

Handfast Point

join the Purbeck Way as it crosses Ballard Down. Follow the path across the down, past a stone seat and turn right down a path to Studland. The path eventually turns into a road, keep right and follow the road back to the car park. [See page 15 for information about Studland.]

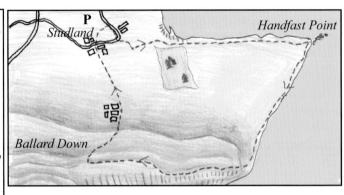

Starting point:
SZ 038826
Distance:
6.5km/4m
Pub: The
Bankes Arms
Notes: Little
climbing, keep
dogs on leads
near sheer
cliffs.

Walk 2 - Corfe Common - Kingston

Follow the road past the National Trust shop to where it stops at Corfe Common [there is a car park along this road]. Alternatively, it is often possible to park at the roadside on the B3069 from Corfe to Kingston, by a gate leading on to the common. Follow the path northwards across the common, up the hill to the village of Kingston. When you reach a wooded path turn right then immediately left, emerging by the **Scott Arms**. Turn left at the road then right at the junction. Climb up the hill and shortly after the old church take a path to the left across the fields. Follow this until it reaches a larger path, the Purbeck Way. Turn left and follow this down alongside a small stream. Continue across Corfe Common, keeping left, and you will emerge at the B3069 again. If you parked in the village go through the gate and over the common to the starting point. There are a number of pubs in Corfe if you prefer your refreshment stop at the end!

Right: In Spring the path behind the Scott Arms is flanked by wild garlic.

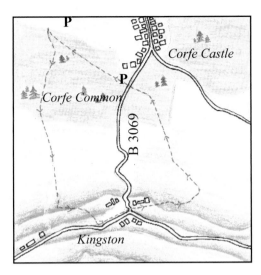

Starting point:
SY 958814 or
SY 963809
Distance: 5.5km/3.5m

Pub: The Scott Arms or
various in Corfe

Notes: A steady climb to
Kingston.

Walk 3 - Kimmeridge

This is a lovely walk to Kimmeridge Bay with the added advantage of free car parking. The walk starts at a small car park in an old quarry on the Chalk ridge overlooking Kimmeridge Bay [SY 918801]. From here go up the road a little way and take the second footpath sign on the left. Follow the path along the ridge. There are lovely views over the bay from here. Just before you come to a stile, take a footpath on the left which leads down the scarp. It can be a little bit overgrown and is quite steep, so be careful! You will soon come to a path on the right signed Kimmeridge Bay; take this and head straight across the fields to the sea [see below]. You will come out on a small road, follow this to the beach.

When you are ready to return, take the same small road back but just before where you came out take the first path on the right. Follow the path across the fields to the road and walk up the road to the church. Go through the gate by the church and follow the path to Top Quarry and the car park.

On the road back to the car park is **Clavell's Café and Farm Shop**. You may

Walks

want to stop here and enjoy some of their local produce. If you want a meal it is advisable to book in season.

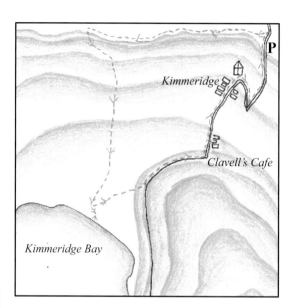

Starting point:
SY 918801

Distance: 4.5 km/3m

Pub: Clavell's Cafe and Farm Shop

Notes: Be careful on short, steep section down from ridge.

Walk 4 – Worth Matravers – Winspit – St. Aldhelm's Head

This walk begins in the lovely village of Worth Matravers, home of the famous **Square and Compass**, a traditional pub frequented by walkers all year round. It takes in the spectacular coastline of St. Aldhelm's Head.

Just below the village pond take the footpath past some cottages and follow it all the way to the coast at Winspit. This was one of the most important quarries of the Purbeck coast *[below]* and was working well into the 20th century. You can explore the old quarry and the huge caves that have been left behind, but please be careful! Just before the old quarry the coast path turns right and climbs up on top of the cliffs. Follow this round to St. Aldhelm's Head. Note the monument to the development of radar here during the Second World War. Take time to explore the little chapel.

Here you have a choice; to the side of the

chapel a gravel road provides an easy path back to Worth Matravers. You can, however, choose the more scenic route continuing along the coast path. The only problem with this route is the very steep valley that you have to descend, then climb along the way. If you wish, have a look at it first before making your mind up! If you choose this way you will be rewarded with wonderful views along the coast and over Chapman's Pool. When you are opposite Chapman's Pool take the path on the right that joins with the gravel road previously mentioned and follow this round back to Worth Matravers.

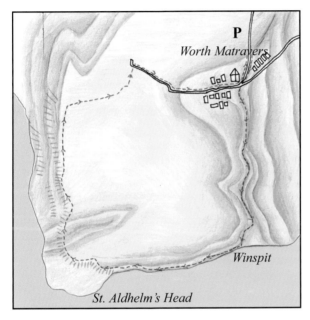

P

Worth Matravers

Winspit

St. Aldhelm's Head

Starting point: SY 974776

Distance: 8km/5m

Pub: The Square and Compass

Notes: One very steep climb which can be avoided if you wish [see text].

Walks

Below: View from St. Aldhelm's Head.

Walk 5 - Kingston - Swyre Head

Follow the small road past the Scott Arms until the tarmac ends. There is a small car park on the left. Go through the gate and follow the path up the hill. At the top keep to the path with the woods on your right and follow it up to Swyre Head. There are wonderful views here both east and west along the coast, east across to St. Aldhelm's Head and west to Kimmeridge, Gad Cliff and the Isle of Portland. Either side of Swyre Head are fertile valleys, each home to impressive estates, Encombe to the east and Smedmore to the west. To return, walk alongside the wall on the west of Swyre Head; go through to the next field, still keeping by the wall, then take a footath on the right signed Kingston and follow this back to the car park. If you wish, make use of the **Scott Arms** on the way out.

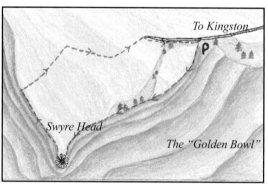

Starting point:
SY 954795

Distance: 3km/2m

Pub: The Scott Arms

Notes: A short, easy walk.

Looking towards St. Aldhelm's Head from the path to Swyre Head.

Purbeck Beaches

I have included some practical information in this guide, but it is largely a personal view of the beaches and their facilities. Purbeck offers a wonderful variety of places to enjoy the sea, from wide, sandy beaches teeming with holidaymakers in summer to quiet rocky coves where, even in the height of season, you can enjoy tranquil beauty. There is plenty of information available from tourist information centres and on the internet. Details will be found at the end of the book.

Studland Beach

Studland
The National Trust looks after the 3 miles of glorious sandy beaches at Studland. You will have to pay for car parking but the facilities are splendid and the beaches broad and ideal for bathing and watersports. The beach slopes gently and is ideal for young children. There is parking at Shell Bay, Knoll Beach, Middle Beach and South Beach. There are toilets at all the beaches and a café, shop and visitor centre at Knoll Beach. There are also cafés at the other beaches. Dogs are allowed except on Knoll Beach and Middle Beach during the height of summer [basically July and August]. South Beach has the added advantage of being next to the Bankes Arms! These beaches are ideal if you want to spend a large part of the day there, relaxing, picnicking and bathing. The car parks provide quick and easy access to the beaches. You can walk, unhindered along the whole stretch of beach, but be aware that there is a dedicated naturist beach at Knoll.

Swanage
For good, traditional seaside fun Swanage is hard to beat. The gently curving bay holds another fine, safe, sandy beach, backed by a promenade. In summer you will probably need to park in one of the main car parks and a little walking may be necessary. There are toilets and a tourist information centre on the sea front and many places to eat and drink within easy reach. No dogs are allowed on the beach from May until the end of September.

Beaches

Winspit

Not a beach as such, but quarrying has left rocky ledges by the water which are ideal for relaxing and listening to the sound of the sea. Great fun to explore the rock pools and clamber over the rocks [but care needed!]. Look out for the fossil of a giant ammonite [Titanites]. Car parking is easy and cheap at Worth Matravers and it is a short walk down to the cove from there. No problem for dogs.

Chapman's Pool

Chapman's Pool is an isolated spot and only reached with some effort. It is not possible to drive there. The best and safest route is to walk south from Kingston. Walk southwards up the road adjacent to the church; it eventually turns into a private track that leads directly to Chapman's Pool. You can descend from the coastal paths either side, but it is steep and often slippery. The best views of Chapman's Pool are from the coastal paths however. If you are energetic it is a good spot to get away from the crowds but still be able to sit beside the sea. Be aware that the cliffs are unstable.

A giant ammonite at Winspit.

Beaches

Kimmeridge

Kimmeridge is famous the world over for its geology, but it is also one of the best places in the UK for diving and snorkelling. The hard ledges of limestone that stretch out to sea provide perfect platforms to explore the numerous rock pools. Kimmeridge is part of a marine nature reserve and the Marine Centre there [open during the summer] provides much advice and information about what to see and where. The beach is rocky but is easily reached from the large car park [toll on approach road payable]. All in all Kimmeridge is a great place to spend a day pottering about and exploring. There are few facilities; toilets near the Marine Centre and a café up the road in the village.

Worbarrow Bay

Worbarrow is a delightful, secluded spot. Part of the army firing ranges, it is only open most weekends and in school holidays [see information about army ranges]. It is most easily accessed through the deserted village of Tyneham where there is ample car parking [donation requested]. A long but easy, level path leads down to the pebbly beach. Bathing is safe but the shore does slope steeply. There are toilets at Tyneham and dogs are allowed. A perfect place for a relaxed day by the sea free from all commercialisation.

Mupe Bay

Another secluded, pebbly beach that requires a walk to reach it, this time around 2km from the car park at Lulworth Cove. Again it is part of the army ranges. It is reached via the coastal path from the eastern end of Lulworth Cove that goes past the Fossil Forest [well worth a visit], although in summer you are likely to find people there who have anchored their boat or yacht in the sheltered waters of the bay. There are no facilities and dogs are allowed. Be aware that there can be dangerous cliff falls, particularly from the Chalk at the northern end of the bay.

Lulworth Cove

One of the best known places on the Jurassic Coast, the beach at Lulworth is very popular in summer. Bathing is safe in the calm, shallow water. Another pebbly beach, there are rock pools to explore at low tide. Dogs are allowed and there is plenty of parking near the Heritage Centre which has interesting displays on local geology and history. There are shops and restaurants in the little village.

Beaches

Tranquil Worbarrow Bay.

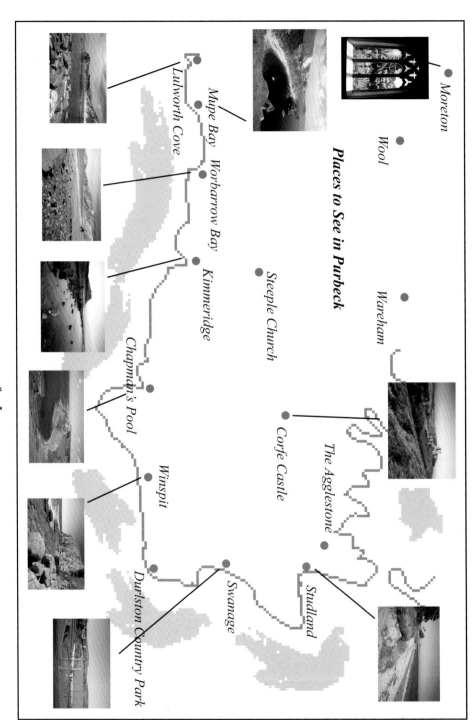

Map of Locations

Places to See in Purbeck

Moreton

Wool

Wareham

Steeple Church

Corfe Castle

The Agglestone

Studland

Swanage

Durlston Country Park

Winspit

Chapman's Pool

Kimmeridge

Worbarrow Bay

Mupe Bay

Lulworth Cove

Hidden Purbeck

Given its relatively small size and popularity with holidaymakers and day trippers, some people might suggest that there is no "hidden" dimension to Purbeck. There are, however, interesting places that are not so well-known and therefore likely to be less well visited than some of the more famous attractions. To those visiting for the first time or not familiar with the area, it is worth pointing some of these out.

At the very north of the region lies **Bere Regis**, once an important, busy town but now more peaceful thanks to the by-pass. Its main point of interest is the church. There has been a church here since Saxon times and the present structure has pieces of architecture from the 11th to the 16th centuries. The magnificent roof of the nave was built in the late 15th century. It contains the tombs of and a stained glass window dedicated to the Turbeville family who were lords of the manor for many generations. It is this family that gave Thomas Hardy inspiration for his novel *Tess of the D'Urbervilles*.

South and slightly west of Bere Regis lies the village of **Moreton**. In the churchyard here lies the grave of T. E. Lawrence,

A detail from an engraved window in Moreton's church.

Lawrence of Arabia as he was widely known. There is a room with mementoes dedicated to him in the village tea rooms. A freak accident during the Second World War was responsible for the homely but ordinary church becoming a truly remarkable place. A German bomber jettisoned a bomb which exploded nearby and shattered the windows. They were replaced by ones engraved by the artist Lawrence Whistler. The effect is truly amazing; the inside of the church has been transformed and each pane is a work of art.

Wool is a thriving and growing community just west of Wareham on the A352. Near where this road crosses the River Frome to the north of the village is another famous site linked to Thomas Hardy. The large house you see is Woolbridge Manor *[above right]*, once the home of the Turbeville family. It was here, according to the book, that Tess and Angel spent the first night of their honeymoon. There is a famous ghostly legend associated with the road that leads north from here to Bere Regis; it is said to be haunted by a phantom horse and carriage, visible only to those with Turbeville blood. For the less superstitious visitor it is also the road to Monkey World!

The Stars and Stripes in the church at Steeple.

Church Knowle is a tiny, charming village with a great pub, on the road to Kimmeridge, just west of Corfe Castle. Carry on this road, past the turning for Kimmeridge and you will soon see a sign on the left to the church at **Steeple.** This picturesque little church has an international claim to fame. In the porch, carved on the wall, is the coat of arms of the Lawrence family who came to Steeple in 1540. A Lawrence had married into the Washington family and a descendant of theirs, George Washington, carried the arms on his signet ring. You will notice that the arms includes "stars and stripes" and is reputed to be the source of inspiration for the first President when he was thinking about a flag for the newly independent nation. So, the flag of the most powerful nation on Earth traces its origins to this tiny Purbeck church! [GR SY 911809]

If you head north towards Wareham and go through the village of Stoborough you will find a turning on the right to **Arne.** There is a car park here run by the RSPB, and a footpath will take you across the heath to **Shipstal Point**. This is a lovely secluded beach on the edge of Poole Harbour. Arne Nature Reserve is a well-known bird watching location; there is an information centre at the car park.

These are just a few of the special places of Purbeck that you might like to visit. Since it is such a compact area it is possible to combine some of these with visits to the more popular attractions such as Corfe Castle, Monkey World or one of the beaches. Something to suit all the family.

Sunset at Shipstal Point on Poole Harbour.

Hidden Purbeck

Background photo - Kingston Churc

Useful Information

Tourist Information
www.purbeck.gov.uk - official site, lots of information
www.visitingpurbeck.co.uk - commercial site but lots of relevant information.
www.swanage.gov.uk
www.VisitSwanage.gov.uk - site of local hospitality association, good place to search for accommodation.

Tourist attractions
Monkey World - near Wool, world famous monkey rescue centre, terrific children's playground.
Tank Museum, Bovington near Wool - amazing collection of tanks, newly refurbished.
Durlston Country Park - at Swanage, spectacular location, frequent events.
Swanage Railway - regular steam and diesel services to Corfe Castle and Wareham.
Corfe Castle - magnificent setting, looked after by National Trust.
Corfe Castle Model Village - very popular with children.
Lulworth Castle - part of the Lulworth Estate, jousting in summer.
The Blue Pool - walks, parkland and tearoom by old clay pit, famous for its unusual and changeable appearance.

All of the above have good websites with full information. Alternatively visit Swanage Tourist Information Centre [on seafront] for details.

Swanage Festivals
Swanage has a number of popular festivals at various times of the year.
Blues Festival - in March and October
Folk Festival - September
Jazz Festival - July
Walking Festival - May [www.walkswanage.com]
Again check websites or Tourist Information Centre for details.

Other useful websites
www.discoverdorset.co.uk - guided tours around Purbeck
www.jurassicjaunts.co.uk - holidays and tours arranged
www.jurassiccoastwalking.co.uk - walking holidays in Purbeck